Control Your Crazy

Work the Good. Tame the Bad and Ugly.

Dr. D. Maria Bivins-Smith, Psy.D.

Correspondence regarding copyright permissions should be directed to:

Wellsmith Psychology, LLC
P.O. Box 1878
Lilburn, Georgia 30047
info@wellsmithlife.com

ISBN 978-1-7322323-0-3 Trade paper
ISBN 978-1-7322323-1-0 Ebook formats

Cover image: Shutterstock.com and is protected by all copyright laws.

To my husband and mom,
my greatest inspirations

Table of Contents

```
well:smith
/wel smiTH/
Noun
    1. One who takes what
    exists and makes it better

Verb
    2. To forge yourself into
    the person you believe you
    can and desire to be.
```

Author's Note

(The information provided in this guide is not intended as treatment for any mental or medical condition or as a substitute for psychotherapy by a licensed clinician.)

A CNN story in 2013 reported that it is the "norm" for many people in Argentina to routinely see a psychologist. Wouldn't it be beneficial if people world-wide felt comfortable talking to a professional trained to help them with their problems, without the stigma?

My mission is to make caring for your mental health, natural and routine, like brushing your teeth, getting treatment for the flu, or managing diabetes.

You have a wealth of knowledge, skills, and abilities. You can flourish in a world that is fast-paced and challenging.

I hope CYC can add some levity and understanding about mental wellness through practical guidance and explanations for living a more peaceful, healthier, and happier life-- on purpose!

Introduction

Advances in research, technology, and medicine are propelling the field of psychology forward with the understanding of how the brain works. These advances are driving the development and fine tuning of ways to help people with mental distress like depression and anxiety and even physical distress for things like pain and hypertension.

I've worked over a decade as a mental health clinician and over 20 years with organizational change initiatives. CYC is based on what I've learned from my patients and clients as well as from my schooling. My knowledge stands on the shoulders of ground breaking scholars, clinicians and practitioners like Aaron Beck, Judith Beck, Albert Ellis, and Arnold Lazarus.

In therapy, the therapist helps people use their brain to learn ways to improve thinking and change behavior to feel better. It's not magic. It's actually your brain making you better. Your brain is made of cells. Thinking and doing things differently changes your brain cells. Changing your brain takes time and patience. However, with persistence you can decrease emotional and physical distress, improve your mood, relationships at work and home, and even decrease pain. Helpful changes lead to better health overall.

You can choose to use CYC as a:

1. Stand-alone guide.
2. Source of inspiration and affirmations.
3. Supplement to your current mental health treatment.
4. Reason to gather with friends for coffee or tea!

The main goal of CYC is that you read, think, laugh, LEARN and GROW!

So, let's go!

<u>Chapter 1</u>

Less Crappy, More Happy

less crappy, more happy

Think about the possibilities. The things you could do if only...

If only what? What holds you back from achieving goals and living a more satisfying life?

Even though we see so many posters, books and signs about "life is a journey," we tend to forget this philosophy when times become difficult and distressful. It's only natural. All of our mental resources go into just keeping on, keeping on. Life's stressful times are well--life!

Your choice to read this book means you are working on you. You are working on making you, better, right now!

You've been on a journey, but has it been "on purpose"?

Well it is now--if you choose it to be!

NOTES

NOTES

Chapter 2

About the Good, Bad, and the Ugly of Crazy

about the good, bad, and the ugly of crazy

You've probably heard some sort of saying that goes, "The definition of crazy is doing the same thing over and over and expecting different results." But what if "crazy" is just being a perfect, mistake making with flaws—human being. So, the good, bad, and ugly of crazy are part of us as human beings.

What if we can let go of the stigma attached to crazy and accept the good, bad, and ugly? Could we feel better about ourselves, when we are not perfect? What if a more helpful way to think about the "crazy" in our lives is just coping? Sometimes, we cope in ways that are helpful. Sometimes we cope in ways that are hurtful, harmful, or not really beneficial.

Here's the thing. Most of us have been learning by getting it wrong since we were born. We didn't start walking until we had plopped on our butts many times. And, we could not even walk until we figured out the crawling thing. Go way back to being in a crib. How many tries did it take to even roll over? Do you get the picture?

We learned from our mistakes to walk, ride a bicycle, add and subtract, and make a friend.

But life didn't stay that simple. Marriage, divorce, jobs, children, disease, disasters, death, substance abuse--life grew complicated as we grew up. And with life's complications sometimes, "the crazy" can get out of control.

NOTES

Chapter 3

Your "Good" Thing or Let's Get Crazy!

your "good" thing or let's get crazy!

Have you ever heard stories about someone who has an idea which everyone said was crazy and just could not be done? Do you remember learning about the Wright brothers and their flying machine? How about the idea of going to the moon? At some point the ideas seemed ludicrous. At one point, it was considered heresy to consider the earth revolving around the sun.

If inventors and scientists had not let their imaginations run free, countless creations, inventions, and discoveries would never have been realized. It was the so called crazy thoughts that led to creativity and innovation.

Now consider artists like painters, clothes designers, musicians and of course comedians. Comedians use their "crazy" to make others laugh. Artists can use their crazy to be original and create beauty, awe, and good times. (Think Prince and the song, *Let's Go Crazy.*)

When the crazy is working "good," it can be helpful and fun. It can be used to inspire humor, creativity, to promote bravery, curiosity, exploration, invention, and to entertain, and innovate. We are able to take our life experiences, including the painful and use them to improve, grow, and move toward our full potential. As I said, that's when the crazy is working "good."

You can work on your good thing to reduce your distress and increase your happiness.

But, before you move on, complete the questions below.

Control Your Crazy

1. Name one difficulty you have which
   you want to improve or have been
   working to improve.

   _____

   _____

   _____

2. How do you imagine you would feel if
   that problem went away or lessened?

   _____

   _____

   _____

3. What will you be able to do
   differently if things changed?

   _____

   _____

   _____

NOTES

NOTES

<u>*Chapter 4*</u>

Down the Path of Unbalanced Crazy

down the path of unbalanced crazy

Sometimes the crazy can get out of control, especially when a good thing turns bad and ugly. It's not hard to recognize when the crazy is out of balance and feels bad or has some bad consequences.

Do you recognize some of the symptoms?

Place a check near your experiences.

stressed out__	problem friendships__	neck pain__ Diabetes__
can't sleep__ Gaining weight__	can't keep a job__ Headaches__	high blood pressure__ Disorganized Workplace__
can't lose weight__	crying__	chronic sadness__

disorganized home__	digestive problems__	chronic worries__
problem relationships__	back pain__ poor decision making__	chronic negative thinking__

When crazy turns ugly, it can tend to look like:

arguing	using illicit substances	legal problems
physical fighting	no relationships	bad luck
too many cigarettes	can't keep a job	blaming others
too much alcohol	can't keep a home	chronic health problems
blaming the world		

Most people feel distressed when they find themselves going down the path of the "bad" and "ugly." The distress you feel is a consequence of the bad and ugly.

You can choose to embrace your crazy. You can accept you have the potential for all of it, the good, bad, and ugly. Purposefully, you can use the opportunity to make choices that are helpful to "tame" the bad and ugly. Taming the bad and ugly accepts that those parts of us exist. We can then deal with behaviors that can be problematic, instead of trying to wish, ignore or worse, punish them away from ourselves.

Work

Chances are you have already done many things in your life to help tame
your bad and ugly.

Write down five things you have done to reduce your distress.

_____

_____

_____

_____

_____

NOTES

NOTES

<u>Chapter 5</u>

The Big Head "But"

the big head "but"

When someone tells you something positive about yourself do you hear yourself saying in your head or out loud, "Yeah, but…" followed by a list of your negative qualities? How about when there is every good reason to believe that you can succeed at something new--that voice in your head goes "Yeah, but…" followed by many reasons why you won't be successful?

It's important to recognize the "Big Head But" when you hear your voice in your head. It may prevent you from believing you can change. Just like an actual head butt, it can knock you backward, slow you down, and get in the way of your progress.

Work

1. Does this happen to you?

2. How many times a day do you find yourself saying "Yeah but…"

3. Have you been saying "Yeah, but…" while reading this book?

Notes

<u>*Chapter 6*</u>

It's Not Magic, It's Your Brain (AKA make your own brain matter!)

it's not magic, it's your brain (aka make your own brain matter!)

Like I said in the introduction--it's not magic that changes your life, it's your efforts. It's your choice to change what you think and do. Do you wonder why you keep going back to your old ways? Do you realize that when you try to change, you are actually changing the physical structure of your brain?

And you wondered why it seems so hard to change? That's because it is!!

Since the brain is responsible for all we do, sense, think, and feel emotionally, it's beneficial to understand how the brain accomplishes this task.

So, here goes a one minute or so neuroanatomy lesson. (Oh no! Stay with me. It's only a minute!!)

- In the brain there are fats, proteins, chemicals, and specialized cells.

- They work together through chemical and electrical reactions.

- Specialized cells called neurons grow and connect as we learn.

- Specialized chemicals (e.g. neurotrans-mitters) help this process as well as contribute to how we feel emo-tionally.

- The cellular connections are like well-worn paths.

- Those paths started being etched, even before you emerged from the womb.

- New thoughts and new behaviors accomplished over time make new "paths." Forming new paths allows us to change old, unhelpful habits to new, more helpful habits.

- Our brain changes in this manner to help us remember the new things we learn. Changing is about learning-- forming new paths in our brains.

So it's not magic that changes your life, it's your choices to take the small steps that will actually change the physical structure of your brain. It's you, making you, better!

Work

Do you remember the problems you wrote down?

How many times have you gone back to doing the same old thing?

Does that seem crazy to you?

If you said yes, remember, it's normal to have difficulty changing! Maybe it's not so crazy?

NOTES

NOTES

Chapter 7

The ABCs of Making You, Better

the abcs of making you, better

Upon beginning therapy, I introduce clients to a cognitive-behavioral model of change, the ABCs, a model my clients find useful and easy to understand: **A**ction, **B**rain, and **C**onsequences (adapted from Ellis and Dryden, 1987).

The model flows like this:

Action : When something happens around us or to us. =>

Brain: In our brain, we think. We have thoughts about the action. =>

Consequences: These are the consequences of our thoughts which include doing behaviors, experiencing emotions and having feelings in our body.

We can *choose* to have helpful and healthy consequences versus hurtful, harmful, and hindering consequences.

Example: CASSIE
Action: Cassie's boss yells at her.

Brain: In Cassie's brain she has thoughts about her boss like: She's disrespecting me. I hate to be disrespected.

Consequences: Cassie is really angry (emotion.) Her stomach is in knots (bodily feeling.) She curses her boss out and then quits her job. (behavior)

In the example above, Cassie's boss did not "push her buttons" nor did the boss *make* Cassie quit. Cassie had thoughts before her behavior. (She's disrespecting me. I hate to be disrespected.) It was her thoughts that made her angry. It was her anger that led to the possible hurtful choice of quitting a job.

Now let's look at Cassie use her thoughts in a different way in another example:
Action: Cassie's boss yells at her.

Brain: She has thoughts about her boss. (She's disrespecting me! I want to curse her out. Don't curse her out! I might lose my job. She must be having a nervous breakdown. I'll be silent. Maybe I'll tell human resources...) **C**onsequences: Cassie feels angry (emotion) She says nothing. (behavior) Cassie keeps her paycheck.

Notice in the second example how many more things Cassie said to herself to end up with helpful consequences. Although she still felt angry, she was able to think her way through the difficult situation of being mistreated. Perhaps she will quit in the future—maybe after she has another job lined up!

In the Action-Brain-Consequences model, there is one area in which we can have a high impact to change our behaviors and our emotions. The area is *our* brain. We can change the thoughts in it. The model assumes if we can become aware of our thinking, we can make **CHOICES** to **CHANGE** how we think and thus, improve the Consequences.

Sometimes thinking habits can keep us in a rut. We end up with the same hurtful and sometimes harmful consequences. Importantly, psychologists work to help you overcome unproductive thinking habits that may be difficult to accomplish alone.

NOTES

NOTES

Chapter 8

Handle Your Own Biz

handle your own biz

Many times, I have encountered people looking for answers to change other people around them. They often feel frustrated, angry, depressed, and anxious over their lack of success. The ABC model demonstrates that change can begin with what we can control--our thoughts and behaviors. We have the ability within ourselves (our brains) to change ourselves, our situations, and our lives. Using this ability effectively becomes empowering. Sometimes, others will respond with changes of their own because YOU CHOSE to do something different.

Work

Are there some people you wish would change their behaviors?

Write down a behavior you wish (write in a name)_____would change.

_____

_____

Write down two things you could say to yourself to deal with _____'s behavior.

1._____

_____

2._____

_____

Write down two things you could do differently to help yourself deal with _____'s behavior.

1._____

_____

2._____

_____

NOTES

Chapter 9

WARNING: Your Brain Will Fight to Stay the Same

warning: your brain will fight to stay the same

I want to set a realistic picture for you. Retraining your thinking to be helpful in achieving your life goals instead of hindering your goals is difficult. Your brain will fight to stay the same.

Your brain has developed many neural connections that have "wired" in the way you currently think. You will try over and over again to find reasons why you can't think or do things differently. Your brain does not want to change! You might feel some frustration. (Remember the "Big Head But"?)

Why is this? Well, it's probably because change brings uncertainty. Our brains like things to be predictable because to our brains, uncertainty means danger. Our brains are made to protect us. Changes might mean danger. So, we naturally may work hard to stay the same, so we can protect ourselves—even when it's not helpful to our best interests.

Work
Name one habit you were successful with changing?_____

How long did it take?_____

What did you tell yourself in order to make a desired change?_____

NOTES

<u>Chapter 10</u>

The Fear Response: Fight, Flight, or Freeze

the fear response: fight, flight, or freeze

Our brains evolved to keep us safe. You've probably heard of the fear response of fight, flight, or freeze. Parts of our brains, together with hormones and other organs evolved to help us survive. Our bodies get in ready mode to keep us alive.

Think of animals that automatically freeze, run or attack when scared. Humans have the same quick responses to danger.

Now here is the tricky part. Even though our brain might want us to do the fight, flight or freeze thing, it might not be prudent to do these responses in our day to day life. For example, it probably isn't helpful to run away from your job when you feel anxiety (which triggers the fear response) about the presentation you need to do at work. However, your brain still will produce the fight, flight or freeze response to the situation.

People experience many bodily sensations. These may include sweating, increased heart rate, increased blood pressure, indigestion, nausea, diarrhea, and shortness of breath. You most likely have been successful on many occasions with dealing with these sensations to accomplish a task.

Work

How do you know when you are anxious?

_____

_____

How does your body feel?

_____

What do you do to control your anxiety?

_____

_____

What do you say to yourself to calm down?

_____

_____

When was the last time you were successful
with controlling your anxiety?

_____

_____

You most likely had success in making
helpful choices in what you think and then
do to control anxiety. You are working to
do these helpful actions on purpose.

NOTES

NOTES

Chapter 11

Choose to Choose

choose to choose

Every day, we make endless choices on what to eat, how to dress, where to go, what time to eat, who to call, what to say and so on. Our choices about what we do during our day are endless.

Do you realize you can and do make choices about what you think, too? Have you ever told yourself, "I'm just not going to think about that right now," or "I'll ignore that for the moment"? You were choosing what to think.

Since you have the power to choose what you think, you *can* choose to think your way into doing what is healthy and helpful. One of the first steps is identifying the thoughts that are holding you back and then taming them with thoughts that are helpful and which move you forward.

Work
Name four choices you made today.
_____
_____
_____
_____

Were any of those choices difficult?
_____
_____

What did you tell yourself to accomplish the difficult choice?
_____
_____

NOTES

<u>Chapter 12</u>

A Tool for the Taming: STOP, BREATHE, THINK

a tool for the taming: stop, breathe, think

Do you think all that yoga, meditation, and breathing stuff is hokey or magic? Nope, again—it's all about your brain.

Remember, your brain is geared toward survival. So, of course getting oxygen into your brain keeps you alive. And it does so much more!

Oxygen or the lack of it tells your body how to respond to stress and when it's time to relax. Is the stressor something big, like a snake? Your brain will know to supply oxygen to the parts of your anatomy so you can run.

However, certain parts of our brain may not be able to distinguish between the type fear of confronting a rattle snake and the fear of giving a speech. So, if we feel fear about giving a speech, our brain will react like the speech is a rattle snake. Heart rate and blood pressure go up. Adrenaline and cortisol surge. The stomach contracts; and blood rushes to the part of our brain for the flight, fight or freeze response-- not very helpful for giving a speech.

But breathing IS helpful. Breathing gets the oxygen flowing again to the part of our brain that allows us to think and reason things out. (Do you remember the neocortex?)Breathing activates the brain to slow down the heart rate and reduce blood pressure. The process causes a physical response, so you can relax.

Work

Go ahead, STOP. BREATHE slowly and deeply two times.

   1. In through the nose. Count: 1, 2, 3.

   2. Out through the mouth. Count 1,2,3,4. (Hold your mouth like you are blowing out candles.

Now, THINK about your relaxation response. (e.g. Slower heart rate, slower breathing, relaxed muscles.)

So now that you understand why breathing works, you can choose to use it to interrupt the thoughts that can lead you down the path of undesired crazy.

   3. Repeat steps one and two.

To learn more about the breathing technique go to Wellsmithlife.com.

NOTES

NOTES

<u>Chapter 13</u>

Think Helpful or Hurtful

think helpful or hurtful

Are you a mean girl--to yourself?!!! (This applies to guys, too!) Do you call yourself stupid, fat, ugly, no good, a failure? Wow. That's not nice! Would you allow your child to talk that way to another child? Most of us would not. We would reprimand our children to let them know their words are unkind and hurtful.

How would it feel if someone called you—-I mean YOU AND ALL YOU DO lazy and stupid. Would you feel good about yourself? I'm going to guess the answer for most people is "no." Most people would feel hurt by those words. Now here's the thing...many people believe they are "motivating" themselves by using hurtful words—toward themselves.

Work

Do you call yourself negative names?
How are those words helpful for you?

_____

_____

How do you feel, when you call yourself negative words?

_____

_____

What holds you back from finding kinder ways to talk to yourself?

_____

_____

How might those words hold you back from accomplishing your goals?

_____

Are you ready to choose something different?_____

What can you say to encourage yourself?

_____

_____

NOTES

Chapter 14

Mind Your Mind

mind your mind

L isten to what you say to YOURSELF. There is a version of a bible saying, "As a man thinketh in his heart, so he is." What do you say about OTHER people? Do you concentrate on the negative qualities of others?

Most people are not perfect. Don't we all make mistakes, have problems, and get grouchy for one reason or another? We are all human beings just trying to do the best we can with what we've got.

Sometimes, we forget that when people behave in negative ways, it's not ALWAYS about us. We can use our brain to choose how we interpret every situation. We can choose to join in the misery, (as misery loves miserable company) or we can choose to find thoughts that are helpful and let them steer us in a path toward feeling and behaving better for the long term.

Arguing, fussing, and fighting might feel good for the moment, but what are the consequences to us, to our families, and to our friends?

Work
List two positive qualities of someone you don't like.

_____

_____

List two reasons someone might act grouchy.

_____

_____

What can you choose to think when someone acts in a bad mood toward you?

_____

_____

What can you choose to do?

_____

_____

How could you use the tool STOP, BREATHE, THINK for helpful consequences?

_____

_____

NOTES

Chapter 15

Powering Up Your Will

powering up your will

Dieting, running a marathon, and accomplishing life's goals are some of the things we associate with the need for the thing called will-power. But when we fall back to old habits or fall short of a goal, the idea that there may not have been enough will-power comes into play.

Do you beat yourself up with the negative chatter in your head when you think you lack "Will Power?"

But what is this power of the will that perhaps only a few have persistent command? The idea of anything requiring power implies that it needs a source of power.

Fortunately, the idea of will-power is exactly that --an idea--a thought. And as we've discussed, it is our brain that enables us to have a will, directs our thoughts toward long-term goals, and helps us to achieve those goals.

But it is the quality of those thoughts that strengthens what we term a will and gives it power. Persistently hurtful and harmful thoughts can weaken the will (i.e. drain our will-power), while helpful and healthful thoughts can strengthen our will-power.

We have millions of cells in our brains dedicated to powering our will. But just like an engine with old dirty oil, too much unhelpful thinking may be gumming up the works.

If you find yourself feeling down or anxious (or both) over the same issues time and time again because you think you don't have enough will-power, challenge the thought. Investigate what you say to yourself every day. That self-talk is a component of what we call will-power.

Are you working on developing healthy habits like eating better or exercising more?

Tame

What are you saying to yourself that is hindering you from accomplishing these goals?

_____

_____

The next time you start on your goal, write down the thoughts. Examine which ones are helpful.

Explore which ones are hindering you. Listen to your reasons for sticking with the thoughts that hinder you.

Write down a date on your calendar in the next week which you will choose the helpful thoughts.

What self-statements can you say to help power your will?

_____

_____

NOTES

NOTES

Chapter 16

Challenge the Negative Chatter

challenge the negative chatter

D o you believe that what you say to yourself is more important than what anyone else says to you?

Just think about it. When someone says something negative to you, you can choose to believe it—or not. You might even argue with someone who criticized you or said something negative about you.

But when you hear your voice in your head saying something negative, do you believe it? Do you believe it 100%? Do you accept it as the whole truth when you hear yourself saying "I'm stupid," or "I'm no

Good?" Do you agree without questioning the thought?

Can you be kind to yourself when you make a mistake? Is any human being perfect? If we are human, we will make mistakes. How you talk to yourself to recover from mistakes is your opportunity for growth and improved well-being. Or, those moments of self-talk can be destructive and limiting. The negative chatter going on inside our own brains can be more destructive and limiting than what anyone else can say to us.

Work
Copy the following statements onto a piece of note paper:

1. No one is perfect.

2. I make mistakes. I forgive me. I'm human.

3. I'm working on it.

4. Stop, Breathe, Think!

NOTES

Chapter 17

Zero to 100 Percent

zero to 100 percent

In Challenging the Negative Chatter, we looked at the idea of believing 100% in the negative thoughts we might have about ourselves.

Now let's look at Suzanne. She comes home from work and says, "I had a terrible day. Look at this house. It's a wreck. My kids are lazy!"

Suzanne is actually telling herself that 100% of her day was terrible, 100% of her house is a wreck, and 100% of the time her kids are lazy. Imagine how she feels with these beliefs--probably pretty miserable.

But Suzanne has the power of her brain. She can choose to balance her thoughts. If she spent eight hours at work, perhaps only 1 hour she spent reworking a report was "terrible." Let's say the rest of her day was "okay." So if Suzanne had a "Terrible" scale she would find that only about 13% of her day was actually terrible and 83% was okay.

0%__>terrible_13%_____>100%

Imagine how much better she could make herself feel if she thought, "Gee, even though one hour was rough, most of my day was okay!" She could even go through the process for her thoughts about her apartment and kids. In choosing to balance her thoughts, Suzanne can actually improve her mood, feel better, and probably enjoy her family more when she gets home from work.

Let's do some more reality balancing for Suzanne with her house…

Suzanne's apartment has three bedrooms, one bathroom, a kitchen, dining room, some closets. Is the entire place a wreck 100%?

Suzanne's a busy woman. She could actually decide to be momentarily satisfied with straightening one room, or just making her bed. Her apartment won't be 100% perfect, but she can bring some joy into her life by choosing to be content with say 10% clean.

0%---10%----------------------100% clean

You can do the same zero to 100% process to balance your thoughts.

Do you say things to yourself like, "I'm lazy" or "stupid" when things aren't going the way you want them to go or when you make a mistake? To your brain, it sounds like you are saying you are these qualities "100%" of the time. The fact is that some days, many people do not feel up to going to work or fulfilling obligations. People get sick, run down, and overworked. That's part of being a human and not a machine. Doesn't that make sense?

Challenge:
What can you say to yourself that is kinder and helpful for motivation?

_____

_____

What are some self-statements you can tell yourself when you don't live up to your own expectations? (Hint: Did you write down the self-statements from the previous chapter?)

_____

_____

NOTES

NOTES

<u>*Chapter 18*</u>

Sometimes Being OKAY is GREAT!!!

sometimes being okay is great!!!

L et's face it, we live in a world of over-stimulation. Video-games, reality TV, soap operas, the daily news all imply life should be an action-packed drama or full of routine happiness and people who look perfect on the outside.

But as you are aware, life is life. Stuff happens. You get sick, you have problems at work, you try to balance a relationship and a career, have break-ups, divorce, experience disasters, and deaths of loved ones. These are natural parts of life. And when these things happen, sometimes just feeling bad can make us feel guilty and terrible about not feeling good! Especially when it seems like no one else can understand our pain.

So, it is really helpful to remember that you are human and human beings get sad, scared, angry, mean, and experience uncomfortable emotions—and that's OKAY. You can give yourself permission to feel bad when people around you may not understand and want you to "get over it."

After giving yourself permission to feel what you feel, then you get to choose how and when you can make yourself feel better.

Remember it takes time to change your brain with helpful thinking, so you can feel better.

Work

What have you been feeling bad or worried about?

_____

_____

Are you ready to work on feeling better?

_____

_____

How soon can you start working?

_____

_____

What can you begin to tell yourself to feel better?

_____

_____

What can you do to feel better?

_____

_____

NOTES

NOTES

<u>Chapter 19</u>

Helpful Thinking Versus Positive Thinking

helpful thinking versus positive thinking

Helpful thinking means balancing where you place your thoughts. Negative thoughts have a purpose. Otherwise, you might try to walk across a highway with cars speeding 60 miles an hour. Too much positive thinking about your ability to accomplish this feat would be a real problem! So, negative thoughts do have their place. Life isn't ALL positive or ALL negative. Accepting that life is not perfect, and we are not perfect is a helpful step toward a more satisfying life. Remember, a question you might choose to ask yourself can be, "Is this thinking helpful?"

Bad things occur to us and we make mistakes. How long we dwell on life's negative experiences impacts us emotionally. We can choose how long and when to dwell on our negative thoughts. There is no magic to erase the thoughts out of our brain. When I work with patients who have negative experiences, we practice how to keep the thoughts about those negative experiences from intruding and ruining the whole day.

Work
Remember when you last became angry with someone.

What thoughts were going through your brain?
_____
_____

What did you feel?
_____
_____

What did you do?
_____
_____

Do you still feel angry (or do you feel yourself becoming angry?)_____

What do you wish you did better?

_____

_____

What thoughts could have been more helpful to reduce your anger?

_____

_____

Tame
How often do you smile in a day?

Practice smiling or deep breathing even when you don't feel like it! Smiling and deep breathing can interrupt the angry thoughts. It is the exact opposite of what your brain expects to continue down the path of unhelpful thinking.

NOTES

NOTES

<u>Chapter 20</u>

Being Happy on Purpose: Generate Some Joy

being happy on purpose: generate some joy

Life has its challenges.

Some days, happiness may not come easy, or at all.

Sometimes, there just seems to be nothing to be happy about. But, how many times are you waiting for someone or something to "make you happy?"

Remember, feeling happy is not magic. It's all about helping your brain learn ways to generate its own joy. When you become down and depressed and things aren't going your way, do you forget about those "little things" in life that bring joy into your life? Taking stock of the little joys of life can generate chemicals in our brains that help us feel joy.

Sometimes being happy takes some purposeful thinking and action on our part. Being happy on purpose requires that you do something to be happy.

You can get prepared for the down times. Make a list of your many joys, blessings, and things for which you can be grateful. Below are three joy generating questions to ask yourself.

Work

List two responses for each question below. Write them down, and put them on a sticky note where you can see them every day. Practice them, so you can be prepared to use them to kick- start your joy and to be happy on purpose.

1. Who are the people in my life for whom I can be thankful?

   _____

   _____

2. What senses do I have for which I can be thankful?

   _____

   _____

3. What abilities do I have for which I can be thankful?

   _____

   _____

Anything else?

NOTES

NOTES

Chapter 21

The Thinking Vacuum (Or Nothing from Nothing Leaves Nothing)

the thinking vacuum (or nothing from nothing leaves nothing)

Concentrating on what you won't do; don't want; can't do, and don't have leaves a vacuum. When you are trying something new, like accomplishing a goal, do you find yourself telling yourself what you are not going to do? Perhaps you want to cut down on the junk food. So you tell yourself, "I won't eat anymore potato chips." Okay. So now what? What will you do instead of eating chips? Do you plan something to replace those chips? What are you going to do when you want those chips…when the voice in your head says go ahead get some of those chips, eat those chips.

Tame

Choose to get your plan together. If you have a plan about how you will handle cravings to go back to old ways, it will be easier to deal with the temptation to revert to old habits.

Include in your plan what you are going to do as well as what you will say to yourself to keep you on track.

1. My goal is … (For example: Walk 20 minutes a day.)

2. I am prepared to address my old thoughts that hold me back by listing them and answering them with helpful thoughts.

For example, I can tell myself how good I am treating my body. I can see myself with a smile and feel great about my accomplishment.

Remember, all your accomplishments start with your brain. Telling yourself (your brain) what you are going to do (the plan) and helpful self-talk as well as visualizing your actions, actually make your brain change in ways to help you be successful.

You... AND improved!

NOTES

Chapter 22

I don't want to be like my mother (or father, sister, brother, etc.)

i don't want to be like my mother (or father, sister, brother, etc.)

The thinking vacuum can deeply impact us. It's an amazing thing to me, how I've had patients tell me they never wanted to be like their (mother, father, etc) but now they find out they are behaving in the same way! I can see the distress it causes them. After spending so many years guarding against behaving in ways they thought were detrimental or dysfunctional, they find themselves exhibiting the same problematic behaviors. How could it have happened?

From the time you left the womb, you started learning how to interact with the world from the people closest to you.

Doesn't it make sense that you will act like the people you learned from as you grew up?

Tame
To prevent a problem behavior, you can choose a helpful behavior to replace it. What problem behavior are you trying to prevent?

_____

_____

What behavior can you choose to replace the problem behavior?

_____

_____

It is also helpful to look at all the beneficial qualities you have learned from someone you are "trying not to be." It is unlikely that the person you are trying not to be had zero positive qualities and all (100%) problematic behaviors.

Name two positive behaviors someone you do NOT like has.

_____

_____

Work

What personal qualities do you want to have?

_____

_____

What accomplishments are you striving to achieve?

Write three sentences regarding how you want to act toward others (e.g. kindness, respect, humor).

1._____

_____

2._____

_____

3._____

_____

Imagine someone will introduce you to a theater full of people.
Write 3 sentences describing what you would like the person to say about you.

1._____

_____

2._____

_____

3._____

_____

NOTES

NOTES

Chapter 23

Now, Just Where Are Those Buttons?

now, just where are those buttons?

Do you ever say, "So-and-So knows how to push my buttons," or "He/she makes me mad?"

Take a look at yourself.

Do you see any buttons on your body?
Of course, you don't. But how many of us use this phrase when we talk about someone "making me" angry or upset?

Often, how we feel happens so quickly, we don't even realize that it's our own thoughts **about** what someone says that makes us feel the way we do.

Next time you think you had your buttons pushed, stop and think about what you were thinking. You can choose to feel or not feel a certain way. That is your power working.

Tame

Remember the time someone did something to you that you did not like.
How did you react?

_____

_____

What thoughts were going through your brain at the time?

_____

_____

What could you have done differently?

_____

_____

What could you have thought differently to help you feel better?

_____

_____

(Hint: I'm going to breathe and let her act foolishly all by herself!)

NOTES

<u>Chapter 24</u>

Break the Brain Chains

break the brain chains

The kinds of thoughts that can weigh you down and bring you down emotionally could be looked at as Brain Chains. The thoughts are not problems. They become problematic when they are used in ways that distort reality.

One type of brain chain are beliefs which people commonly say to themselves about the way things "should," "must" or "need to" be. Thoughts become brain chains when they succeed in making you believe that you don't have a choice. The reality is you have choices and your choices have consequences.

Every day we all make choices to do things that help us succeed or hurt our success.

You can choose to go to work, or not. You can choose to take care of your children or not! Of course, choices come with consequences. But when you understand that you get to choose the paths you take in life, you can feel unburdened by the often unwritten rules we subject ourselves to every day. And you can feel good about some of the difficult choices you make to help others and yourself.

Tame
Do you have rules about how you think you or other people "should" behave or what they "should do?"

Write two of them down.
1._____

_____

2._____

_____

Work
Next time when you hear yourself saying what you should or must do, and you're feeling sad or depressed, or overwhelmed over it, ask yourself, "Who made that rule?"

If the answer is "I did," then you're the one who can change it or accept it—but now you get to choose it!

NOTES

Chapter 25

Free Yourself: Sneaky Brain Chains

free yourself:
sneaky brain chains

Remember, brain chains are the kinds of thoughts that can weigh you down and bring you down emotionally—just like wearing a heavy chain. There are many types of brain chains. But what they have in common are their consequences. These thoughts can make you feel worried, anxious, trapped, angry, and even overly suspicious. Remember, brain chains can distort reality. Brain chains are sneaky because we use the words every day.

All or none thinking/Generalizations
Do you hear yourself saying words like always, never, every time, everyone, no one, or no-body?

Sylvia is at work. Her boss has a frown. She says to her coworker Martin, "My boss is always in a bad mood."

If you're Martin, would you believe Sylvia?

Think about it? Is Sylvia with her boss 24/7? It is very unlikely Sylvia knows her boss's mood 100% of the time. But her statement implies she "always" knows her boss's mood.

Tyrone says to his friend LaVaugh, "Get your girlfriend flowers. All women like flowers."

Do you think Tyrone knows "all" women? Perhaps Tyrone's girlfriend will like flowers, but his statement is a generalization. Maybe *many* women like flowers, but Tyrone certainly doesn't know what "all" women like.

Discounting

Do you hear yourself saying "yeah but" when you hear something good? Do you then think about all the negatives—and then no longer count any of the positives?

Catastrophic Thinking

When you try to do something different or set a new goal, do you hear yourself thinking about all the bad things that might happen?

Mind Reading

Do you worry too much about what other people think—even strangers?

It is an important part of getting along with others to make guesses at what other people think. However, when our guesses are mostly negative, there may be a brain chain at work.

Are you living your life persistently worried about what everyone thinks about you or what you are doing?

What are the consequences of your thinking this way? How do you feel emotionally and physically?

_____

_____

What could you say to yourself to balance the negative thoughts?

_____

_____

NOTES

NOTES

Chapter 26

Confusing Wants with Needs

confusing wants with needs

The only thing you "need to do" is breathe. Everything else is a choice. Hmmm? Do you believe that premise?

Okay, I'm not going to ask you to hold your breath until you pass out. But, if you did, there is a high probability that once you pass out, you will automatically start breathing again.

So, with breathing (as well as the other autonomic functions like our heart beating) we do not have control, therefore no choice in the matter.

Every day you get up and make choices. It's your decision to deal with your life. It's your power to push through those tough days, take care of yourself and your family. It's your choices that get you through the day, no matter how difficult.

Distress can stem from believing you have no choice in what you do. Clients have said to me. "I don't have a choice. I have to go to work." The reality is, there will be consequences for actions (e.g., unexcused absences from work will likely get you fired.)However, a choice is being made. A choice to go to work results in helpful consequences (e.g., a paycheck, the ability to pay rent, buy food.)The choice to not go to work results in harmful or hurtful consequences.

When you acknowledge your tough choices every day, you get to be responsible for you. You also give yourself the deserved credit for making the tough, uncomfortable, or inconvenient choices.

Work

Write three tough, tiring, or difficult choices you made today. (Hint: Did you take your medication, exercise, not eat fried chicken, bring the kids to their event, or drink only one glass of wine?)

1._____

_____

2._____

_____

3._____

_____

NOTES

NOTES

<u>Chapter 27</u>

He should, she should, and they should... Who made that rule?

he should, she should, and they should... who made that rule?

Do you ever hear yourself saying what someone else "should" do? Here's an example. Sylvia did not get a promotion that she worked very hard to obtain. She lamented a long time that she should have been promoted to the job and that the process should be fair at work. She became so disgruntled that she began to act out with a poor attitude and poor work quality. She felt justified, like she was getting back at someone. Eventually, Sylvia lost her job.

Many of us have developed rules for ourselves, others, and the way the world "should be." The reality is that there is no rule book for many of the ways that we tend to believe people should behave (e.g. fairness).

Of course, it would be a great world if people only followed the rules like being fair, polite, respectful, and reciprocating our kindness and love. However, we are all different with different values. What's fair to me, might not be so to you. We don't ALL see the world the same way.

Usually, we feel pretty crummy when people don't live up to the rules we have for how we believe other people should behave. Feeling upset and sad when we are let down is normal. Most of us don't enjoy being let down. However, acting out in unhelpful ways toward others at work and in our families can lead to unhelpful and hurtful consequences.

Work

There are some signs that you might be getting jammed up because you have some rules you believe others "should follow."

Has a supervisor, someone at work, friends, or family complained you have a problem with your attitude? Yes No

Did you feel angry or upset after being told this news?

Tame

What can you tell yourself when you feel let down, sad or angry to help yourself feel better?

_____

_____

What helpful thoughts can you say to yourself to help yourself feel better?

_____

_____

Write down some of the beliefs you have about how people "should behave."

_____

_____

NOTES

NOTES

Chapter 28

Are you "Shoulding" all over yourself?

are you "shoulding" all over yourself?

Are you terrorizing yourself with "I should do this and I should do that? Again, you can ask yourself, "Who made that rule?"

You probably learned to tell yourself what you should and should not do to get some helpful consequences. For example, "If I want to have strong bones, I should drink milk;" or "If I don't want to go to jail, I shouldn't rob a bank;" "I should work, if I want to buy nice clothes."

Making rules for ourselves can be helpful. Rules become distressful when we stop realizing we are making a choice in following any rule, even our own. Acknowledging that we are making a choice allows us to purposefully consider our actions.

I've had clients who have been very upset because family members persistently borrowed money from them. But, then the family member never paid them back. The client would lament they felt taken advantage of. However, that did not stop them from giving their money away. They had a rule: "If I have the money, I should share it." The client's experience of giving someone else their money, and then not having the money to do things they wanted to do was very distressful. The situation became the source of stress, arguments, and resentment in the family.

Work

Can you relate to having the "SHOULDS"?

Do you have your own rules that end up making you feel anger, resentment, depressed, anxious?
Name one.

_____

_____

What thoughts do you have about what others will think or do if you break your own rule?

_____

_____

What would the consequences be for you if you broke your own rule?
Emotional_____

_____

Feelings in your body

_____

Do you CHOOSE to accept the consequences of following or not following your rule?

_____

_____

NOTES

NOTES

Chapter 29

Grow up and Be You (Self-Esteem and Self-Confidence)

grow up and be you (self-esteem and self-confidence)

Self-Esteem and self-confidence are based on how people think about themselves. How often do you hear yourself lamenting or complaining about what you can't do versus what you can do? How do you think about you? Do you have old unhelpful thoughts running your life? Do you still hear your parents' (or relatives, teachers, etc.) negative or limiting ideas about you from when you were a child in your head? Do you think about your future in terms of what you don't want to be?

Control Your Crazy

Isn't it time to let you be you?

Aren't you a grown up, now?

It's your brain and your choice to change those old thoughts. You can change those old thoughts to your OWN thoughts.

Challenge: Say to yourself 5 positive qualities that make you who you are today.
1._____
2. _____
3._____
4._____
5. _____

List five of your accomplishments. (No matter how small, you did it!)

You are a survivor. You are a Thriver!
1._____
2. _____
3._____
4._____
5. _____

NOTES

Chapter 30

Making LIFE S.E.N.S.E.

making life s.e.n.s.e.

There are some basics for emotional well-being. These include getting sufficient sleep, exercising, and eating healthy. Saying what to do, as many of us experience is easy. It's the doing that can be challenging. But if you can schedule, you can organize your way to better health and overall well-being.

An easy way to remember these basics is about making **SENSE**:
Scheduling
Exercise,
Nutrition
Sleep/**S**upport
make you **E**xcel!

At the beginning of every day, prioritize these activities in your schedule, so you can excel. Scheduling requires PLANNING and PRIORITIZING.

Give your tasks/activities a time of day to get them done. You can use your phone calendar, notes in your phone, paper stickies on the fridge—whatever works for you! Then, ask yourself, "How CAN I do this?" How CAN I get this done?"

You can't make time, but you can take the time to get what you can do, done!

Work
Ask yourself, "How **can** I get at least fifteen minutes of exercise (If you haven't started yet.)

_____

_____

What's one healthy thing I **can** do each day for my nutrition?

_____

_____

How **can** I get seven to eight hours sleep?

_____

_____

Remember:
Take small steps!
If you fall, you CAN get back up and keep moving forward.

Note: There are many books written about organizing your day. You can jump start planning. Make a list of what you want to accomplish for the day at the beginning of each day. Then prioritize what is important. Set times to get the tasks done. You can break big tasks into small ones by deciding what you can get done in 15-minute increments.

NOTES

NOTES

<u>Chapter 31</u>

Doing Is Believing

doing is believing

Can you do just a little bit of something? Do you tell yourself it's not worth doing if you can't be perfect or if you can't do it 100% the way you "think" it should be done? Remember, it's your thinking that can thwart you from accomplishing your goals.

Remember, making changes may trigger a fear response of fight, flight, or freeze. When you find yourself procrastinating or avoiding change, your brain may have you in a "freeze."

Your brain may be producing thoughts to keep you from experiencing distressful emotions like embarrassment and rejection.

Do you recognize any of the thoughts below?

___ No one will like that.

___ Everyone will laugh.

___ You're not good enough, yet.

___ You're going to fail.

All of the above may happen, but you will survive! Your brain is designed to protect you from being hurt. Feeling embarrassed and rejected won't kill you! But your brain might be telling you otherwise to keep you from feeling distressed.

Work
When you are in a "freeze," mode (procrastinating or avoiding) remind yourself: "My brain is trying to protect me from changing."

1.Write down a time when you procrastinated completing a task that would have helped you achieve a goal. (Or, what are you procrastinating with, right now?)

_____

_____

2.Write a statement to challenge each of the statements below to help you work with your fear. (Hint: This might take re-reading a few past chapters.)

i. No one will like that.

_____

ii. Everyone will laugh.

_____

iii. You're not good enough, yet.

_____

iv. You're going to fail.

_____

Tell yourself: "It's okay" to take small steps toward my goal.

Examples for the answers to the above:

-Not everyone has to like it. Someone may like it.

-I won't figure out how good I am until I try.

-I'm working to succeed. Failures are lessons for future success.

NOTES

NOTES

Chapter 32

No Such Thing as Thought Police (well yet...)

no such thing as thought police
(well yet...)

In sci-fi movies you may have seen or heard of, there are the thought police. However, at this time, they don't exist. You are free to think what you want. When it's still in your brain, it's no one's business.

And just as you are free to think what you want, you are free to feel whatever emotion that arises in you. But here's the thing, emotions don't stay just in our head. Other people typically can see them.

We cry, laugh, shout, turn red, and pout. Sometimes emotions are hard to hide.

Then comes the part when someone says, you "shouldn't feel that way."

Well, just like your thoughts, you have a right to feel what you feel. Your feelings are *your feelings*. They are not right or wrong. They just are. You have a right to feel what you feel. You're a human being, after all! Human beings have emotions.

What may become problematic is where, when, with whom, and how you demonstrate your feelings. There will probably be very different consequences for yelling because you're angry at your boss at work and yelling at your child at home. Even though we have a right to our feelings, it is *our behavior* that counts.

Work
When was the last time you were angry?

_____

_____

What was going through your head at the time?

_____

_____

Did you try to challenge any of those thoughts?

_____

_____

How could you have challenged those thoughts?

_____

_____

What's helpful in dealing with feelings is understanding what thoughts provoked those feelings in the first place.

NOTES

NOTES

Chapter 33

Ditch the Comparisons

ditch the comparisons

How often are you comparing yourself to others? How do you feel when you don't measure up to the other person? It's normal to look at others and compare ourselves. But just because it's normal does not always make it helpful to our sense of well-being. Sometimes a little comparison is helpful, but too much can be harmful. When you feel inspired to do more or reach for your goals a little harder, then comparison is probably helpful. When you feel resentment, jealousy, anger, depression, or anxiety, then comparing yourself to someone else is probably hurtful, at best.

I've seen the quote attributed to Theodore Roosevelt that "comparison is the thief of joy." Comparison is a two-sided coin. You can let it steal your joy, or you can let it spur you on to greater achievement, like when someone works hard to break a record in sports.

Tame
List one time you compared yourself to someone else and did not measure up.

_____

_____

How did you feel when you did not measure up?

_____

_____

Were you inspired to do more?

_____

_____

Did you feel distressed?

_____

_____

Set your goals to be the best you.
You can practice gratitude for what you have, while still seeking more.

NOTES

Chapter 34

You Have the Right to Refuse, Rectify and Request

you have the right to refuse, rectify and request

I cofacilitated an anger management group during one of my externships. One thing my supervisor would tell the group was, "You have the right to refuse, rectify, and request."

He explained that you have the right to
1) Say no (Refuse);

2) Ask for what you want someone to do or not do (Request);

3) Change your mind (Rectify.)

Sometimes, we feel angry when we do not refuse, request, or rectify. For example, we say "Yes" when we wish we had said no. Or we wish people would do something or not do something. Other times, when we think about some of our decisions, we want to change a commitment, but we choose to let the situation remain. These actions or lack of actions may lead to us feeling angry, anxious, and over the long term, even depressed.

We can't control what people ask of us and what people do. But, we can choose our response. When we don't feel in control and believe we are "obligated" to respond in a certain way, we may feel angry with ourselves and others.

Are you looking to change?

It is likely that our own thoughts about the consequences of saying no or asking for what we want, keeps us from saying what might be more helpful to our own well-being.

Tame

How often do you say yes, when it would be more helpful for you to say no?

_____

What thoughts do you have when you think about saying no?

_____

_____

Is there something you fear will happen?

_____

_____

A very helpful response to a request of you is, "Let me get back to you."

By delaying your response, you give yourself time to think and deal with your options and thoughts.

This leads to the next brief chapter…

NOTES

NOTES

<u>Chapter 35</u>

Step Away from the Crazy

step away from the crazy

Who said you must react and deal with everything when it happens?

You can step away and deal with it later when you have your thoughts together.

NOTES

NOTES

Chapter 36

Sleep Like a Baby

sleep like a baby

Question: When you are sleeping what can you *do* to solve any problems you were having during the day?
Answer: Absolutely nothing!

So, sometimes for some of us and all the time for many of us, our brains will work 24 hours a day, if we let them. Our brains were made to keep us safe and solve any problems that might put our safety in jeopardy.

But again the question, what's the one thing we *can* do when we are sleeping to solve our problems.
Answer: Sleep!

Control Your Crazy

Anxiety, depression, concentration and memory problems, weight gain, high blood pressure, diabetes, and a list of other medical problems are worsened by lack of sleep.

Again, use your own brain to soothe yourself and convince yourself to get at least 7 hours of sleep.
Note: Waking up at night is normal. Our sleep cycle was made for us to be able to go to the bathroom and ensure our safety.

Sample Plan for Sleep.
1. Use the bathroom right before you get into bed. Limit liquids 2 hours before going to bed.

2. If you have a busy brain, write down your to-dos. Tell yourself they will be okay until the morning without you.

3. Turn off the television, computers, and phones.

4. Eliminate or cover light sources. (e.g., computers, cell phones, clocks, chargers, etc.)

5. If you awaken, tell yourself it's okay to go back to sleep.

6. Work on limiting pets in your bed.

What three (or more) things can you do to promote better sleep?

1. _____

   _____

2. _____

   _____

3. _____

   _____

Physicians can prescribe you medication to assist you with sleeping. But did you know you can find psychologists and other mental health professionals who are trained to help you with sleep hygiene.

If you don't have success on your own, you may benefit from help from a professional.

NOTES

NOTES

Chapter 37

Why a Mental Health Professional?

why a mental health professional?

I t can be pretty confusing about whom to go to for help.

It is beneficial to get professional mental health treatment for problems that are causing you distress (anxiety, depression, insomnia, chronic pain, substance use, etc.) Mental health professionals are individuals who have received training in accredited school programs, have an advanced degree (e.g., Master's and Doctors) AND are licensed by the state in which they practice.

I'm a psychologist. So I will speak from the standpoint of what I know about my profession.

In most states, psychologists have a doctoral degree of Ph.D. or Psy.D. They must complete more than 90 hours of coursework. Many complete over five thousand hours of clinical training experience before they are allowed to take national and state exams. After passing the exams, they can obtain a license to independently practice psychotherapy (therapy) and be called a psychologist.

Psychologists are trained to diagnose and treat mental illness with clinically based approaches (approaches that have been used in professional treatment settings like a hospital or clinics) commonly termed as "talk therapy." Cognitive Behavioral Therapy (CBT) and various Psychoanalytic therapies are just a few of the approaches psychologists use to help clients/patients reduce distress. These approaches, as I discussed throughout this book, help people change how they think and behave, so they can feel better.

Although psychologists do not prescribe medicine in most states (see note), they are trained to understand the biology of mental illness, use biological based interventions to reduce stress (e.g., deep muscle relaxation) as well as understand the impact of medications on mental illness diagnoses.

People with schizophrenia and bipolar disorders often get treatment because of the serious and extended nature of their problems. But, if you experience repeated and extended periods of distress and dissatisfaction with your life, then seeking the services of a psychologist may be indicated.

Some examples include:

- Repeated periods of depression/sadness

- Ongoing problems with maintaining a job and/or relationships

- Suicidal thoughts

- At least one Emergency Hospital visit for suicidal thoughts

- At least one Emergency Hospital visit for symptoms which you thought were a heart attack and were diagnosed with "Panic" or "Anxiety" attacks.

- A history of suicide attempts or thoughts

- At least one psychiatric hospital-ization

- Difficulties with reducing substance or alcohol use which lead to health, employment, and relationship problems.

- Difficulties with following recommended medical treatment for problems like diabetes, high blood pressure, chronic pain, or obesity.

If you are or have been experiencing any of the above, the help of a psychologist can assist you toward mental as well as overall wellness. You can check to see if the mental health provider has experience with working with your problem.

NOTE:
Psychiatrists, who are medical doctors (M.D.) and other medical professionals (e.g. Nurse Practitioners) write prescriptions for psychiatric medications. There are states in which specially trained and licensed psychologists prescribe psychiatric medications.

NOTES

Chapter 38

Final Note: The Last Little Crazy Bit

final note: the last little crazy bit

Mental wellness goes hand-in-hand with your overall health.

Remember, when you're distressed, you may want to check in with your crazy. Is it out of balance? Are the bad and ugly out of control?

Tame it and then work it!

Now that you've reached the final chapter, you can take the opportunity to skim for 5 minutes through the chapters you've read. What chapters were most meaningful to you? Take this time to write down your top ten chapters.

_____

_____

_____

_____

_____

_____

_____

_____

_____

_____

Choose to read each one of these chapters again over the next 10 days.

And just in case you missed them, here are self-statements that can help reduce your frustration with yourself and others.

1. I'm working on it.

2. I'm taking small steps. Small steps get me there.

3. I forgive me.

4. I'm human.

5. No one is perfect.

It's helpful to have some control tools.

Do you have yours yet?

_____ Calendar (Cell phone, Wall, book)

_____ Scale

_____ Stickies

_____ Index Cards

You get to control you. Your greatest power to change is in your very own brain.

You can make you, better!

NOTES

Follow Dr. Bivins-Smith on Wellsmithlife.com and Facebook

Wellsmith your life and make you, better!